# ACCOUNTING ACQUAINTANCE

## An Introduction to Accounting: Theory and Practice

**ONYERHOVWO KATHERINE ERAKORO AKINBOLA, I.C.I.A.**

**ACCOUNTING ACQUAINTANCE**
**AN INTRODUCTION TO ACCOUNTING: THEORY AND PRACTICE**

iUniverse books may be ordered through booksellers or by contacting:

iUniverse
1663 Liberty Drive
Bloomington, IN 47403
www.iuniverse.com
1-800-Authors (1-800-288-4677)

Because of the dynamic nature of the Internet, any web addresses or links contained in this book may have changed since publication and may no longer be valid. The views expressed in this work are solely those of the author and do not necessarily reflect the views of the publisher, and the publisher hereby disclaims any responsibility for them.

Any people depicted in stock imagery provided by Getty Images are models, and such images are being used for illustrative purposes only.
Certain stock imagery © Getty Images.

The views expressed in this work are solely those of the author and do not necessarily reflect the views of the publisher, and the publisher hereby disclaims any responsibility for them.

ISBN: 978-1-5320-9522-1 (sc)
ISBN: 978-1-5320-9523-8 (hc)
ISBN: 978-1-5320-9524-5 (e)

Library of Congress Control Number: 2020902858

Print information available on the last page.

iUniverse rev. date: 04/24/2020

# Contents

# Dedication

*This book is dedicated to the Terrestrials and Clusters, for immense blessings upon me.*

# Introduction

*This book contains about accounting in its pure form. It entails basic and perfect accounting orientation to anyone who wants to learn about accounting in a simple and focused manner. It's about just being able to have an approach and being able to have a look into what it is with accounting. It's actually knowing about something in an introductory formant, it does not contain actual advanced details or internal advanced details of putting together accounting statements, although accounting statements are presented in advanced state for introductory discussion, as this book is a theory introduction of accounting.*

*If you have wondered about pure accounting this book will be of help to you to have a good idea of what it is. Accounting as it is does need very many numerous rigorous studies, mastering and practices to fully understand, this book is just only one of it that you can look into to get some help from. I welcome you to read this book and get it to introduce you to accounting excellently. If you are already use to accounting and are just looking to gain more help the pure details of accounting in this book can also be of help at some level, even in doing actual accounting work.*

*This book also mildly discusses accounting in finance and business. There are some accounting terms that do have meaning in accounting that are different from its other general use outside the field of accounting, some of these accounting terms are explained in accounting definitions in this book for understanding. This book gives a good knowledge and introduction into catching a view of accounting.*

*This book has been written with very strong accounting background, I am an accredited member of the Guild of I.C.I.A. Canada, and also a College Accounting Graduate, I have perfected Advanced Accounting practices and Management. I Major in Accounting at Thompson Rivers University, Kamloops, British Columbia, Canada, and am an associate member of Chartered Accountants of Ontario, Canada. I am also a College graduate Toronto, Ontario, Canada where I concentrated on Payroll Administration. Also am a Member of Canadian Payroll Practitioner. I graduated from High School in Nigeria and i hold a postsecondary certificate in Accounting from University of Benin, Nigeria. I am also a member of Institute of Professional Managers, London, England. I have done numerous extensive researches on Financial Accounting, Economics, Equities, among others and has excellent accounting knowledge and experience in preparing Accounting statements and reports.*

# Ackowledgement

I want to thank Terrestrials and Clusters for kindness, love, mercies and numerous blessings upon me.

My dear Parents helped me so much all the way to make this book a reality. I want to thank my Father for his care. I want to acknowledge my Mother for encouraging me, building my confidence and believe for what is good.

Everyone who has helped me has been of very much help to this book. I want to thank my brothers for their outstanding inspiration; especially I want to thank Ochuko O. Erakoro for his excellent intelligence in the social science's inspiration with me. I want to also thank my sisters for their support.

All my indispensable friends indeed you shine in me like gold. Thank you my friends very much.

I very well remember, and I want to thank my colleagues, teachers, lecturers, professors and Instructors who have helped me all the way and who have refined me into an Accountant.

I want to commend Akinola A. Akinbola,(ICAN) for his expertise, Akinbola has studied in Post Graduate Degree in University of

*Glasgow in Glasgow, Scotland, United Kingdom in international finance and he is a member of Institute of Chartered Accountants of Nigeria ICAN, member. I want to appreciate my lovely son Afunre Akinola A. who is easy to write this book at home with to make this book a success.*

*Thank you everyone very much.*

# About the author's academic and profession

*Onyerhovwo Katherine Erakoro Akinbola, I.C.I.A. is an accredited member of the Guild of I.C.I.A. Canada. She is also a College Accounting Graduate, where she perfected Advanced Accounting practices and Management. She Major in Accounting at Thompson Rivers University, Kamloops, British Columbia, Canada. Onyerhovwo is an associate member of Chartered Accountants of Ontario, Canada. She is also a College graduate Toronto, Ontario, Canada where she concentrated on Payroll Administration. She is a Member of Canadian Payroll Practitioner 2010. She graduated from High School in Nigeria and she holds a postsecondary certificate in Accounting from University of Benin, Nigeria. Onyerhovwo is also a technician member of Institute of Charted Accountants of Nigeria ICAN before proceeding to North America and has continued Accounting.*

*Onyerhovwo is also a member of Institute of Professional Managers, London, England.*

*Onyerhovwo has done numerous extensive researches on Financial Accounting, Economics, Equities, among others and has excellent accounting knowledge and experience in preparing Accounting statements and reports. Onyerhovwo works in the accounting sector and has her Accounting Company in Canada that does preparation of Accounting Reports and Accounting Statements, Payroll, and Tax.*

*Onyerhovwo is the founder and President in Management of a Beauty Pageants, Toronto, Ontario, Canada, an Organization which organizes beauty pageants, to build self-esteem and confidence.*

*Onyerhovwo has been married and has children.*

# Chapter 1

# ACCOUNTING DEFINED, THEORY AND PRACTICE

*The term __accountancy__ is sometimes used to refer to __accounting,__*
*Accounting is the action or process of keeping financial accounts*

reports and accounting is the language of business. It is the system of recording and summarizing of financial transactions pertaining to a business, the process of summarizing, verifying, reporting the results and analyzing, accounting reports are used for decision making by decision makers, directors, investors, board members and governments. The financial statements that summarize the operations of an organization, the financial position of an organization and its cash flows over a particular period of time such as weekly, monthly or annually are a summary of numerous financial transactions entered into over the actual financial period being reported. Depending on an organization's management style and certain variances, a day's financial report can be created where necessary. Accounting is one of the key functions for almost any business.

Some field of work sometimes have terms used pertaining to its professionals understanding that do often times have meaning that are entirely different in other usage outside of it to other type of work professions and users. There are some accounting terms that do have meaning in accounting that are different from its other general use outside the field of accounting, some of these accounting terms explanations are in the following accounting definitions.

Some of the functions of accountants

Accountants function in very large varieties of performances in the financial accounting sector and the social sciences field. Accountants also keep the accurate records or recording of financial accounting data and reports, deals with an organisation or a firms financial operations and also individual accounting record statements where necessary. Accountants' also give financial accounting advice to the organization as financial reports for an organization management use. Often times *these financial accounting advice when utilized, results in very high growth and development of the organization.*

*Account is a type of method of recording and summarising the transactions of businesses.*

*Account in balance or Account balance is a type of account record which increases and decreases to equal the account.*

*Accounting equation is the basic equation to show the relationship in the accounts between the assets, liabilities, and owner's equity of a business. The fundamental equation is:*

*Assets=Liabilities +Owner's Equity*

*Example:*

**Theory Introduction**

**Canadian Edition**

*$5,000,000 Company's assets = $3,000,000 Company's liabilities+ $2,000,000 Company's owner's Equity*

*Accounting period is the period that is covered in an accounts statement. Accounting period is a full year circle for an organization. Sometimes a shorter period exists. Shorter accounting periods are often a day or a week period of time, a month period and quarter periods are all shorter accounting period in comparison to the basic annual or year period of time which consists the of 12 months of the year.*

*Accounts payable account is the controlling account in the general ledger used to put together all creditors and summarise all accounts with creditors in a separate accounts payable ledger.*

*Accounts receivable account* is the controlling account in the general ledger that puts together receivables and summarizes all of the accounts with customers in a separate accounts receivables ledger.

*Accrual basis* is the method of keeping accounts that shows all expenses incurred and income earned for a specified period of time, even though such expenses and income may not actually have been paid or received in cash during this specified period of time. Accrual basis consists of actual income and expenses of a period of time and the anticipated income and expenses of the same period of time, all added together and subtracted together as necessary, sums the accounts of accrual basis.

*Accrued expense* is an expense incurred but has not been paid off.

*Accrued income* is income already earned but has not been collected.

*Accrued interest* is interest incurred or interest earned depending on the circumstance or type of transaction at hand and has not been paid or has not been collected depending on the type of transaction as applicable until the next period.

*Accrued salaries* are salaries that are owed to employees by employer for one period but not paid until the next.

*Accumulated depreciation* or *Allowance for depreciation account* is the account to which estimated depreciation accounts are added.

*Adjusting entries* are entries that are made in the general journal at the end of an accounting period to bring some accounts up to date.

*Allowances for bad debts* are the reserve for bad debts, allowance for bad debts account is the account used to show the estimated loss expected on credit granted. It can be shown as an offset against the value shown for accounts receivable.

*Asset is whatever thing that is of value owned and used by an organization.*

*Authorised capital stock is the actual total amount of stock that a corporation is permitted to issue.*

*Bad debts are debts that are receivables in accounts receivables but are not collected or are not paid by debtors after a long period of time.*

*Bad debts collected are bad debts in accounts receivables that have been written off as not collectible but that are later paid by debtors.*

*Bad debts expense is not to be anticipated, but where it occurs, bad debts expense is the expense account to which the amount of the loss on uncollectible accounts is debited to.*

*Balance sheet is a financial report at the end of an accounting period to give a detailed actual report of the financial condition of a business as of a specific date. The balance sheet is sometimes referred to as the statement of the financial position of an organization.*

*In the balance sheet of an organization the total liabilities amount show the amount of resources that are financed by creditors.*

*The balance sheet is based on the accounting equation as it pictures the fundamental link between assets, liabilities and owner's equity.*

*In practical form an example of a balance sheet is presented in figure 1.1.*

*Example:*
*Figure 1.1*

## Theory Introduction

## Canadian Edition

### Bede Company
### Balance Sheet
### August 31, 20XX

| Assets | | Liabilities and Owner's equity | |
|---|---|---|---|
| **Current assets:** | | **Current liabilities:** | |
| Cash | $100,000 | Accounts payable | $20,000 |
| Marketable securities | 70,000 | Interest payable | 5,000 |
| Accounts receivable | 110,000 | Total current liabilities | $25,000 |
| Merchandise inventory | 400,000 | | |
| Prepaid insurance | 10,000 | **Long-term Liabilities:** | |
| | | Note payable due | |
| Total current assets | $690,000 | January 31, 20XX | 20,000 |
| | | Total long-term liabilities | 20,000 |
| **Investments:** | | | |
| Investments in securities | 105,000 | **Total liabilities** | 45,000 |
| | | | |
| Total investment | 105,000 | **Owner's Equity:** | |
| | | Ony Bus Capital | 1,320,000 |
| **Property, land and equipment:** | | | |
| Land | 70,000 | | |
| Building | 400,000 | | |
| Equipment | 60,000 | | |
| Total property, land and equipment | | | |
| | $ 530,000 | | |

| Intangible assets: | | Total Liabilities and | |
|---|---|---|---|
| Patents | 40,000 | | |
| Total intangible assets | 40,000 | | |
| Total assets | $1,365,000 | Owner's Equity | $1,365,000 |

As seen in figure 1.1 a balance sheet clearly sums the all assets items, fixed assets, current assets, investments assets were applicable and if there is, it also includes all intangible assets, all liabilities whether long term or current liabilities and the owner's equity of a firm or in some instances of an individual. Land, property and equipment are fixed assets.

(Continuation of accounting terms explanations in accounting definitions.)

Bank statement is a detailed record of all checks cleared and of deposits made plus the ending balance of an account with a bank.

Bond is a method of borrowing money through an interest bearing negotiable instrument.

Budget is the estimate of future income and expenditure of a specified period of time.

Comparative balance sheet is a balance sheet containing information for more than one accounting period, in order to use all the accounting periods' balance sheets in comparative analysis.

Cumulative preferred stock is a form of preferred stock that accumulates the claim for unpaid dividends from year to year.

*Current assets* or *liquid assets* are assets in the form of cash or are assets that can be converted to cash within a short duration of within one year. Practical examples of current assets that can be found in the current assets accounts and depending on the type of organization and depending on the asset capacity of the organization in variables ranges are:

## Theory Introduction

## Canadian Edition

*Cash $*_____

*Prepaid insurance* _____

*Merchandise inventory* _____

*Supplies on hand* _____

*Accounts receivables* _____

*Note receivables* _____

*Marketable securities* _____

*Note: The above are core current assets as they are often cashed and or used up as applicable within a year period of time.*

*Corporation business are the type of businesses that deals with Marketable securities.*

*Current liabilities refer to liabilities that are to be paid in a short period of time in a year. Practical example of items in the Current liabilities accounts are:*

## Theory Introduction

## Canadian Edition

*Salaries payable $_____*

*Wages payable _____*

*Interest payable _____*

*Taxes payables _____*

*Accounts payables _____*

*and other current debts or other current liabilities.*

*Note: The above sets of payables are very short term in dealings and are as such regular short term debts. So they are examples of real current liabilities.*

*Depreciation is the decrease in the value of fixed assets due to wear and tear, in the passage of time, and obsolescence.*

*Dividends refer to the portion of the earnings of a corporation distributed to the stockholders.*

*Equity is the value amount of a total claim against the assets of a business.*

*Expense in accounting is a decrease in ownership resulting from the operation of a business.*

*Expenses include items such as wages, rent, advertising cost, travel, delivery cost, supplies used, taxes paid, insurance purchase, repairs cost and utilities.*

*Fee* is a charge that is made or paid depending on the transaction for services rendered.

*Fixed assets* are assets that are useful for more than a year period of time. Fixed assets are long term assets with a long-term durability value. Practical examples of fixed assets in fixed assets accounts are:

## Theory Introduction

## Canadian Edition

*Building* $_____

*Land* _____

*Machinery* _____

*Factory* _____

*Equipment,* _____

*Development site and other fixed assets.*

*Note: Building, land, machinery and equipment are primary fixed assets as land is a fixed property in nature and machinery and building also equipment do last a long time in use as assets and as assets capital.*

*Fixed liabilities* or *long term liabilities* are liabilities that are not due for payment for over a year period of time. Some long term liabilities are of Instalments payments over a long period of time, some are not to be paid by instalments payments but do have a long future due dates depending on the type of organization and depending on the item, transaction variability, and method of acquiring the account item.

*Practical example of long-term liabilities in long-term liabilities accounts are:*

**Theory Introduction**

**Canadian Edition**

*Note payable $ _____*

*Mortgage payable _____*

*Bonds payable _____*

*And other fixed liabilities or long-term liabilities.*

*Note: The above sets of payables are actual long term in specific and are typical long term debts or liabilities and are very good examples of long term liabilities.*

<u>*Gain on disposal of fixed assets*</u> *is the gain of income generated when a fixed asset is sold for more than its book value. The book value amount minus the actual amount which a disposal item was sold at, if there is an income generated, the income generated becomes a gain on the item in the fixed asset that is disposed.*

<u>*Goodwill*</u> *refers to intangible asset representing the difference between the book value of a business and its sale price.*

<u>*Gross income*</u> *is the total income of a business before taxes.*

<u>*Honored*</u> *is when a draft or note is paid or accepted.*

<u>*Income*</u> *is the increase in owner's equity.*

*Income statement* refers to a statement that shows all the items of income, all items of expenses, and the net income or the net loss depending on the actual situation, for a specified period of time. A practical example presentation of an income statement is in figure 1.2.

Income statement actual purpose is to show the operating results of an organization for a specified period of time, as shown in figure 1.2 a month's income statement. The net income is derived from the excess revenue over expenses.

*Example:*
*Figure 1.2*

**Theory Introduction**

**Canadian Edition**

*Tig Trading*
*Income Statement*
*For the month ended January 31, 20XX*

| | | | |
|---|---|---|---|
| *Sales* | | | *$ 50,000* |
| *Cost of goods sold* | | | *21,000* |
| | | | |
| **Gross profit on sales** | | | *29,000* |
| **Operating expenses:** | | | |
| **Selling expenses:** | | | |
| *Sales salaries* | *$ 7,360* | | |
| *Advertising* | *1,200* | | |
| *Travel* | *1180* | | |
| *Delivery* | *700* | *$ 10,440* | |
| **General and administrative expenses:** | | | |
| *Office salaries* | *4,010* | | |
| *Taxes* | *1,100* | | |
| *Insurance* | *400* | | |
| *Supplies materials* | *150* | | |
| *Utilities* | *600* | *6,110* | *16,550* |

| | |
|---|---:|
| *Total operating expenses* | *12,450* |
| *Net operating income* | *<u>100</u>* |
| *Other income* | *12,550* |
| *Other expenses: interest* | *<u>600</u>* |
| *Net income* | *<u>$ 11,050</u>* |

*(Continuation of accounting terms explanations in accounting definitions.)*

<u>*Intangible assets*</u> *are assets of intangible nature such as goodwill, patents and copyrights. In the accounting structure intangible assets do appear in the assets accounts practically in instance where there are only two items of intangible assets owned by an Organization, it will possibly be presented in the assets accounts as follows:*

## Theory Introduction

## Canadian Edition

*Intangibles assets:*

*Patents $ _____*

*Copyrights _____*

*Total intangible assets $ _____*

*Note: The above intangible asset account is an actual typical list of what an intangible asset account or actual intangible assets are.*

*Interest* refers to the amount of money that is charged a borrower for the use of money.

*Interest expense* is the expense that is incurred for the payment of interest on any form of debt.

*Interest income* is the income realized from interest on accounts receivables and other accounts.

*Interest rate* is the percentage which shows the relationship between the interest for a specified period of time and the principal amount.

*Investments* in assets accounts are investments in securities, land held for future site and other form of investments that are purchased for future appreciation.

*Liability* refers to an amount that is owed such as debts, accounts payables, and long term debts or long term liabilities.

*Liquid assets* or *current assets* are assets in the form of cash or are assets that can be converted to cash within a short duration of within one year.

*Liquidation* is the process of selling all assets of a business to pay liabilities, with any remaining funds distributed within the owners of the business.

*Long term liabilities* or *fixed liabilities* are liabilities that are not due for payment for over a year period of time.

*Market value* refers to the actual value amount at which a share of stock can be sold at a specific time.

*Maturity value* is the amount that is to be paid when a note becomes due with interest or without interest.

*Miscellaneous entries* are entries that are not to be recorded in a special journal and are recorded in the general journal.

*Net income* is the difference derived when income is larger than expense.

*Net loss* is the difference in decrease when expenses are larger than income.

*Operating expenses* refers to the costs that are incurred by a business that shows a decrease in the ownership with exception of expenses incurred represented by the cost of goods sold.

*Operating income* refers to the increase in owner's equity of a business from its principal operations.

*Owner's equity accounts* is the capital equity summary comprising of retained earnings, net income and drawings or withdrawer by the owner. Sometimes depending on the organization the equity includes stock dividends and dividends, various stocks such as preferred stocks, common stocks and their percentages and price per value.

*Partnership business* is a type of business organization in which two or more persons come together to form a business and share in operating the business together in agreement and share profits or losses of the business.

*Payee* is a person or a business that a payment is paid.

*Payroll* refers to a list of employees that are entitled to payments of salaries or wages for a particular period with the amounts of each employee of all employees on the list.

*Payroll taxes* or *employment taxes* are taxes collected on salaries and wages of employees.

*Petty cash fund* is an amount of money that is kept on hand for making payments of small amounts of cash to operate a business or for use.

*Reconciliation statement* is the actual balanced reconciliation statement after the process of bringing into agreement the balance of a bank statement and the balance on check stubs.

*Retained earnings* are the amount of money that is earned by a business and is in hold in the business and not given out as earnings but kept as surplus earnings or accumulated earnings.

*Revenue* refers to the inflow of assets which result from conducting the activities of a business.

*Revenue expenditure* refers to a certain expense or expenditure that do not increase the value of a fixed asset but which is useful in maintaining the asset in good operating condition.

*Sales budget* refers to the estimate of the income anticipated from sales for some future period of time.

*Sales tax* is the tax a seller of commodity must collect on sales to customers and in turn remit the sales tax to the government as applicable.

*Salvage value* is the amount for which a fixed asset is sold at the end of its approximated useful period.

*Solvency* is a company's ability to pay up debts as at when due.

*Stakeholders* are those who own part of a business capital or part of a working capital of a film.

*Statement of account* refers to a form which is sent to a customer that shows charges to the customer account with amounts credited to the account and showing the balance of the account.

*Stock certificate* is a document evidence of a stockholder's ownership in a corporation.

*Stockholders* refer to the individuals who own one or more shares of stock in an organization often time a corporation type of organization.

*Stockholders equity* is the capital stocks account summary comprising of retained earnings, stock dividends and dividends, various stocks such as preferred stocks, common stocks and their percentages and price per value.

*Subsidiary ledger* refers to a separate ledger summarized in a single controlling account in the general ledger.

*Terms of sale* refers to the agreement made between the buyer and the seller as to what manner of payment to be used in the transaction and the delivery of commodities.

*Trade discount* is the deduction in price from the list of price.

*Trial balance* is the proof of the equality of debits and credits in the ledger.

*Unit record* is a card that contains one complete record.

*Voucher system* refers to a method of controlling disbursements of cash providing that a form be prepared and approved before cash payment is made.

*Withdrawals* are assets taken from the business by the owner of a business for personal use.

*Worksheet* refers to an analysis paper that shows provision for sorting and interpreting the trial balance on a single sheet of paper from which the income statement and balance sheet are prepared.

# Chapter 2

# ACCOUNTING, CAPITAL
# AND FINANCE

*Accounting statements and reports are prepared following the* **generally accepted accounting principles**, *the* **current accounting standards**.

**Conceptual work in accounting** *follows accounting guidelines and accounting methods which are* **objectives of financial reports**

*and accounting reports, qualitative method of accounting information, elements of financial statements, Measurement, and Traditional assumptions of accounting model.*

*The conceptual work in accounting deals with the maintaining the Objectives of financial reports and accounting reports or statements and what these accounting reports and statements have to demonstrate, also what the Qualitative method of accounting information consists, as well what the elements of financial statements require compounds of, along with what the Measurement consists of, and what consists the Traditional assumptions of accounting model. Accounting process deals with the following eight recoding phase's steps: Analyzing business documents, Journalizing transactions, Posting to the ledger Accounts, Preparing a trial balance, Preparing adjusting entries, Preparing financial statements, Closing the nominal accounts and Preparing a post–closing trial balance. Financial statements analysis comprises of items among following proper detailing of these list: Financial statement analysis, Common size financial statements.\, Return on equity, Fixed asset turnover, Margin, Accounts receivable turnover, Turnover, Debt to equity ratio, Cash flow adequacy ratio, Earnings per share, Dividend payout ratio, Book to market ratio, Times interest earned and Number of sales in inventory.*

*The **conceptual work in accounting** consists of the maintaining of;*

***Objectives of financial reports and accounting reports,*** *that statement and reports have to demonstrate the following:*

- *usefulness,*
- *understandability,*
- *evaluating economic resources,*

- *primary focus on earnings,*
- *assessing future cash flows, its actual audience.*

**Qualitative method of accounting information** *consists of:*

- *benefits higher than cost,*
- *be of comparative attributes,*
- *relevance,*
- *reliability,*
- *materiality,*
- *conservatism.*

*The* **elements of financial statements** *require components of the:*

- *assets,*
- *liabilities,*
- *net assets,*
- *equity,*
- *revenues,*
- *investments by owners,*
- *distributions to owners,*
- *comprehensive income,*
- *recognition,*
- *expenses,*
- *gains,*
- *losses.*

**Measurement**, *which consists of the:*

- *historical cost,*
- *current replacement cost,*
- *present value,*
- *net realizable value,*

- *reporting,*
- *current market value.*

**Traditional assumptions of accounting model** *consist of the:*

- *economic entity,*
- *going concern,*
- *arm's length transactions,*
- *the accounting period*
- *stable monetary units.*

**Accounting process of recording**

**The Accounting process** *deals with the following eight recoding phase's steps:*

- *Analyzing business documents*
- *Journalizing transactions*
- *Posting to the ledger Accounts*
- *Preparing a trial balance*
- *Preparing adjusting entries*
- *Preparing financial statements*
- *Closing the nominal accounts*
- *Preparing a post–closing trial balance*

*Choosing to use* **Accrual** *accounting is the choice of an organization and choosing to rather use* **Cash Basis** *accounting is the choice of an organization.*

**The conceptual method for financial statement analysis**

**Financial statements analysis** *comprises of items among following proper detailing of these list:*

- *Financial statement analysis*
- *Common size financial statements*
- *Return on equity*
- *Fixed asset turnover*
- *Margin*
- *Accounts receivable turnover*
- *Turnover*
- *Debt to equity ratio*
- *Cash flow adequacy ratio*
- *Earnings per share*
- *Dividend payout ratio*
- *Book to market ratio*
- *Times interest earned*
- *Number of sales in inventory*

### Opening account

*Most accounting reports or accounting statements give specification on a business cash or capital, the opening money amount at the start of an accounting period. Capital is very important to any business.*

***Capital in definition****: - is money that is invested in a business to generate income. Capital is also described as wealth in the manner of cash on hand or actual assets. Economist definition of capital states that capitals are factors of production that are used in the creation of goods and services and are not themselves in the actual process.*

*Finance is often associated with accounting as it goes hand in hand with accounting.*

*Finance refers to the studies of how people make decisions regarding the allocation of resources over time and the managing of risk.*

*Finance in definition* is the science which states the management, the creation and study of money, investments, banking, credit, assets and liabilities. Finance consists of financial systems, the study of finance and financial instruments, which can relate to countless assets and liabilities. Finance can be categories into 3 parts namely 1, public finance, 2 corporate finance and 3 personal finance, All these 3 parts of finance can contain very many other sub categories of finance.

*Money in accounting* is a unit of accounting measure. *Money* is a legal tender for payment and often is a particular type of currency or currencies at a given time in a place or places which are accepted for the exchange of goods and services. Money is anything of value that is accepted for financial exchange.

*Human capital has to do with the accumulation of investments in people, such investments in people are education, paying for higher education, and training, to increase the human skills productivity in future. With better and effective productivity more value is added and better results are derived.*

*Investment risk*

**Investment risk can be referred to as any risk involved in business investment.**

*Investment risk is often measured by financial business investment risk officers and the risk analysis and or reports are often different pertaining to the particular business or assets value.*

*Currency exchange*

*Currency exchange can the referred to as the exchange of one currency to another.*

*Mostly banks, and or big financial institutions, brokers and forex traders render the commerce and services of currency exchange.*

*The most traded currency is the US dollar and the US dollar is often accepted internationally more easily in exchanges and currency trades.*

*Currency exchange is done sometimes in person and there is a lot of other methods of exchanging currency where accepted.*

# Chapter 3

# BUSINESS ORGANIZATIONS CATEGORISATION

*The Sole proprietorship, partnership and corporation types of businesses are the most common form of businesses.*

The **sole proprietorship** or **entrepreneur organization** is a one person owned type of business.

**Partnership** type of business is when two or more people come together to form a business and share in operating the business together and share its operating capital. Partners also share in gains or loss in the business, they share the business together.

The **corporate type of business** has limited liability, greater capacity of capital, ability to transfer ownership, and continuous existence. The corporate business or corporation is a legal entity and it is responsible for the actions and debts of it. The corporate business shareholders have no personal or legal liability the shareholders are only limited to their share invested in the corporate business capital. As a legal entity, a corporation owns both its assets and liabilities.

**Joint venture** is a strategic alliance where a new entity owned by two or more firms allows the partners to pool their resources for a common good.

Business planning is helpful to the development of a business as business planning is an ongoing process of making decisions that direct the venture in its present objective and in long term success. A business plan generates the decisions that guild the business in its entire form. A further calculative measure of strategic planning when included results to better optimum. Strategic planning as a managerial decision process that matches an organization to its resources and capabilities to the actual opportunities for long-term growth and stability is helpful to an organization for business realization. With operational planning in focus on day to day materializing of the functional plans including detailed yearly, semi-annual and quarterly plans and review a business can possibly grow. When there are competitors a business ability to *outperform and provide customers with a benefit the competition did not, has not provided or cannot provide gives a competitive advantage.*

*The **Not for profit** type of Organization n also exist. **Charities** are other type of organization.*

*A cash flow budget is a type of budget statement or report prepared that explains the anticipated flow if income and revenue to a business or an individual and the anticipated expenses to be made over a specific period of time as listed in the form of budgeting.*

*Having a cash flow budget helps to ensure that you can comfortably pay all your expenses and enables you to manage your revenues and expenses proactively. Strong components include a sales and revenue forecast, anticipated inflows of money, such as accounts receivable, anticipated outflows, such as cost of goods sold, debt repayments, and operating expenses. It is important to keep a cash flow budget very current and to make sure that it reflects changes in your operating business and your plans for your business.*

*Understand the lists in your cash flow such as price, volume, or overheads will have the effective impact on a cash flow. Cost of goods sold in goods and trading business, for example, has a significant impact on a cash flow. At the same time, competitive market may prevent you from increasing prices. Cash flow is also affected by inventory days and accounts receivable days.*

*Manage the credit given to customers by establishing effective credit policies is an important part of successful cash flow management. You might also look for ways to encourage clients to pay more or complete payment quickly. For example, consider discounts for early payments, or charge interest on accounts that are past due. While interest and late charges may actually become a source of income for your business, it's important to apply some due diligence. Extremely late payments are more likely to become write-offs and will also keep some working capital tied up.*

*Keep your payables current by regularly reviewing your accounts payable schedule helps determine how well you are keeping up with your credit obligations.*

*Reduce expenses by looking for ways to cut back without compromising their quality and impact. When business volume rises, bring in temporary, contract, or part time help before committing to additional full time staff. An independent audit may reveal redundancies and inefficiencies that you can quickly look at and plan to improve.*

*Sometimes use from your company's surplus cash flow to work by checking how much money you need to keep aside for emergencies. Review your company's cash flow history for any patterns. As well, consider how potential changes in the economy, such as currency or interest rate fluctuations, could affect your revenues or expenses. Any surplus in your cash flow can be used for business expansion, to pay off debts, or to maintain a certain level of working capital.*

# Chapter 4

# ACCOUNTING REPORTS
# AND STATEMENTS

*Accounting is the language of business. Accounting is also the preparation of financial statements which are also called accounting reports, these financial statements or accounting reports are trading profit and loss accounts statements of businesses, statement of cash flow, income statements, trial balance, balance sheets, retained earnings statements, equity statements, bank reconciliations among others. These accounting statements are not limited to businesses only. Accounting reports are also of the putting together of journals, accounts statements of non-profits, accounting reports of charity organizations,*

*and business equity statements. Accounting reports is also that of individual equity, the recording of petty cash statements of a business with other type of accounting consolidations.*

*Accounting statements are used by organizations management to decide how to improve the business's or organizations financial situations and other findings.*

*Accounting statements also help organizations or individual to know where to make improvements on expenditures and for organization restructuring. Accounting helps the world market, global market to plan ahead and sometimes in order to avoid financial loss. Accounting is often used by Executives, Directors, Managers, Auditor, Accountants, Speculators, Investors, Stakeholders, Potential stakeholders, Governments and Individuals.*

*Management is getting things done by directing and leading people to reach goal and objectives set. With accounting reports organizations are able to function better. As accounting records, statements and reports help managers, executives, board of directors, decision makers and governments to make financial decisions. Accounting reports and statements cannot be underestimated in the business and finance sector as accounting is the foundation and strength to a better economy and development.*

*Services rendering type of businesses do depend on earnings they generate from the provision of services to customers and clients, while merchandising enterprises do depend on earnings or profits derived from the buying and resale of merchandise, commodities or products to customers.*

*Accounting debit and credit entry method*
*Figure 4.1*

## Theory Introduction

## Canadian Edition

| The rules of debits and credits entry | | |
|---|---|---|
| Type of account | Increase | Decrease |
| Asset accounts | Debit | Credit |
| Liability accounts | Credit | Debit |
| Owner's equity accounts | Credit | Debit |
| Expense accounts | Credit | Debit |
| Revenue accounts | Debit | Credit |

*Figure 4.2*
*Example of Post-Closing Trial Balance*

**Theory Introduction**

**Canadian Edition**

*Tig Trading*
*Post-Closing Trial Balance*
*December 31, 20XX*

| | | |
|---|---:|---:|
| Cash | $20,000 | |
| Accounts receivable | 6,000 | |
| Land | 15,000 | |
| Equipment | 18,700 | |
| Accumulated depreciated-equipment | | $ 700 |
| Franchise | 6,000 | |
| Accounts payable | | 10,000 |
| Salaries payable | | 2,000 |
| Tig trading, Capital | | <u>53,000</u> |
| | <u>$ 65,700</u> | <u>$ 65,700</u> |

*Account reconciliation statement is done to reconcile accounts at the end of an accounting period.*

*Income statement shows the state of a business income at a specified period of time.*

*Figure 4.3*
*Example of income statement*

**Theory Introduction**

**Canadian Edition**

*Reve Trading*
*Income Statement*
*For the month ended January 31, 20XX*

| | |
|---|---|
| Net sales | $ 80,000 |
| Other revenue | <u>1,200</u> |
| Total revenue | 81,200 |
| Less: cost of goods sold | <u>(40,200)</u> |
| Gross profit | 41,000 |
| Other expenses | <u>15,000</u> |
| Net income from operations | $ 26,000 |
| Other income | <u>7,000</u> |
| Net income | <u>$ 33,000</u> |

*Figure 4.4*
*Example of income statement with other items such as extraordinary situations occurrence*

## Theory Introduction

## Canadian Edition

*Reve Cooperation*
*Income Statement*
*For the month ended February 28, 20XX*

| | | |
|---|---:|---:|
| Net sales | | $400,000 |
| Cost of goods sold | | <u>280,000</u> |
| Gross profit | | 120,000 |
| Operating expenses: | | |
| Selling expenses | $14,000 | |
| General and administrative expenses | 8,000 | |
| Loss from suspension of work during strike | <u>2,000</u> | <u>24,000</u> |
| Income before taxes and extraordinary item | | 20,000 |
| Taxes (10%) | | <u>2,000</u> |
| Income before extraordinary item | | 18,000 |
| Extraordinary item: <br> Loss from drainage and flood damage | 5,000 | |
| Taxes (10%) | <u>500</u> | <u>500</u> |
| Net Income | | <u>$ 17,500</u> |

*Figure 4.5*
*Extraordinary items are not common in practice. Another example of*
*income statement with extraordinary item*

## Theory Introduction

## Canadian Edition

*Ka Trading*
*Income Statement*
*For the month ended January 31, 20XX*

| | | |
|---|---|---|
| Net sales | | $500,000 |
| Cost of goods sold | | 290,000 |
| Gross profit | | 120,000 |
| Operating expenses: | | 210,000 |
| Selling expenses | $ 16,000 | |
| General and administrative expenses | 10,000 | |
| Loss from suspension of work during strike | 4,000 | 30,000 |
| Income before taxes and extraordinary item | | 24,000 |
| Taxes (10%) | | 2,400 |
| Income before extraordinary item | | 21,600 |
| Extraordinary item: Loss from drainage and flood damage | 10,000 | |
| Taxes (10%) | 1000 | 1000 |
| Net Income | | $20,600 |

*Figure 4.6*
*Example of account balance sheet report*

**Theory Introduction**

**Canadian Edition**

## Tig Trading
## Balance Sheet
## August 31, 20XX

| Assets | | Liabilities and Owner's equity | |
|---|---|---|---|
| **Current assets:** | | **Current liabilities:** | |
| Cash | $400,000 | Accounts payable | $60,000 |
| Marketable securities | 150,000 | Interest payable | 15,000 |
| Accounts receivable | 130,000 | Total current liabilities | $ 75,000 |
| Merchandise inventory | 900,000 | | |
| Prepaid insurance | 32,000 | **Long-term Liabilities:** | |
| | | Note payable due | |
| Total current assets | $1,580,000 | January 31, 20XX | 60,000 |
| | | Total long-term liabilities | 60,000 |
| **Investments:** | | | |
| Investments in securities | 405,000 | **Total liabilities** | 135,000 |
| Total investment | 405,000 | | |
| **Property, land and equipment:** | | **Owner's Equity:** | |
| Land | 100,000 | Ony Bus Capital | 2,700,000 |
| Building | 600,000 | | |
| Equipment | 90,000 | | |
| Total property, land and equipment | 790,000 | | |

| *Intangible assets:* | | | |
|---|---|---|---|
| Patents | <u>60,000</u> | | |
| | | | |
| <u>Total intangible assets</u> | <u>60,000</u> | | |
| | | | |
| | | **Total Liabilities and** | |
| **Total assets** | <u>$2,835,000</u> | **Owner's Equity** | <u>$2,835,000</u> |

*Figure 4.7*
*Example of Statement of Owner's Equity*

## Theory Introduction

## Canadian Edition

*Ka Trading*
*Owner's Equity*
*For the Year Ended December 31, 20XX*

| | |
|---|---|
| K. Ka Capital December 31 | $ 1,000,000 |
| Add: Net income | <u>90,000</u> |
| Total | 1,090,000 |
| Deduct: withdrawal | <u>12,000</u> |
| K. Ka, Capital December 31 | <u>$ 1,078,000</u> |

# Chapter 5

# EQUITY AND SUMMARY

*With efficiency scarce resources can be optimized, equity is a fair distribution of benefits of resources among members. Economics studies the method in which scarce resources are managed, it study how people work, how they make decisions, what they prefer to buy, how much they save and how they invest their savings. In economics price elasticity of demand, is used by markets as the percentage change in unit sales that results from a percentage change in price. Elastic demand is the demand in which changes in price have large effects on the amount demanded. Breakeven analysis is a method for determining the number of units that a business must produce*

*and sell at a given price to cover all of its costs. Example of the use of branding strategies method in managing product has been of help to brands in growth promotion. Branding strategies develops brands and gives value. Equity of an organization in good state demonstrates the use of fair strategies.*

*In a corporation stockholder's equity consists of the amount invested by its stockholders for the shares of the capital stock that have been issued by business corporation and the amounts that has been earned by the corporation in revenue which have not been distributed to stockholders. This corporation amount revenue earned also referred to as profits is decided as to its distribution to the stockholders as dividends.* **Stockholders equity** *is the capital stocks account summary comprising of retained earnings, stock dividends and dividends, various stocks such as preferred stocks, common stocks and their percentages and price per value. Stakeholders are often times investors who own part of a business capital or part of a working capital of a film. Statement of account can be classified as a form which is sent to a customer that shows charges to the customer account with amounts credited to the account and showing the balance of the account.*

*Stock certificate is classified as a document evidence of a stockholder's ownership in a corporation. Stockholders refer to the owners who own one or more shares of stock in an organization often time a corporation type of organization.* **Owner's' equity accounts** *is the capital equity summary comprising of retained earnings, net income and drawings or withdrawer by the owner. Sometimes depending on the organization the equity includes stock dividends and dividends, various stocks such as preferred stocks, common stocks and their percentages and price per value.*

*Example*
*Figure 5.1*

**Theory Introduction**

**Canadian Edition**

*Bede Company*
*Statement of Owner's Equity*
*For the Year Ended December 31, 20XX*

| | |
|---|---|
| B. Bede Capital December 31 | $ 1,000,300 |
| Add: net income | <u>80,000</u> |
| Total | 1,080,300 |
| Deduct: withdrawal | <u>40,000</u> |
| B. Bede, capital December 31 | <u>$ 1,040,300</u> |

*Example*
*Figure 5.2*

## Theory Introduction

## Canadian Edition

*Tig Trading*
*Statement of Owner's Equity*
*For the Year Ended December 31, 20XX*

| | |
|---|---|
| *T. Tig Capital December 31* | *$ 970,000* |
| *Add: net income* | *120,000* |
| *Total* | *1,090,000* |
| *Deduct: withdrawal* | *150,000* |
| *T. Tig, capital December 31* | *$ 940,000* |

*Example*
*Figure 5.3*

**Theory Introduction**

**Canadian Edition**

*Ofori Company*
*Statement of Owner's Equity*
*For the Month Ended August 31, 20XX*

| | |
|---|---|
| *O. Ofori Capital August 31* | *$ 80,000* |
| *Add: net income* | *4,600* |
| *Total* | *84,600* |
| *Deduct: withdrawal* | *1,220* |
| *O. Ofori, capital August 31* | *$ 83,380* |

*Example*
*Figure 5.4*

**Theory Introduction**

**Canadian Edition**

*Val Company*
*Statement of Owner's Equity*
*For the Month Ended August 31, 20XX*

| | |
|---|---:|
| *V. Val Capital August 31* | *$ 60,000* |
| *Add: net income* | *17,000* |
| *Total* | *77,000* |
| *Deduct: withdrawal* | *1,100* |
| *V. Val, capital August 31* | *$ 75,900* |

*Stockholders equity refers to the capital stocks which detail the retained earnings, stock dividends and dividends, various stocks such as preferred stocks, common stocks and their percentages and price per value. Stakeholders are the investors who own part of a business capital or part of a working capital of a film. Statement of account entails a form which is sent to a customer that shows charges to the customer account with amounts credited to the account and showing the balance of the account. Stock certificate is classified as a document evidence of a stockholder's ownership in a corporation. Stockholders refer to the investors who own one or more shares of stock in an organization often time a corporation type of organization. Owner's' equity accounts is the capital equity summary comprising of retained earnings, net income and drawings or withdrawer by the owner. Sometimes depending on the organization the equity includes stock dividends and dividends, various stocks such as preferred stocks, common stocks and their percentages and price per value.*

*Accuracy*

*Total accuracy or complete accuracy is required for accounting.*

*Accuracy in accounting, this area has to do with the correctness of all figures and of all totals. Accuracy in this area also has to do with putting the correct entry of item in its correct accounting area. For example or to illustrate this very well, I will use Assets entry and identification to illustrate this application, Assets are always required to be properly and correctly identified and be entered correctly in always in areas where assets entries are applied and assets must be entered correctly like every other accounting entry, It is not just only the identification of assets that is required is also the entry of the correct figure or amount expertly as applicable, doing very adjustments at every applicable entry and calculating all correct pert ages and interests or all other required applicable calculations to each and every entry as correctly needed in the accounting.*

*The use of Assets to illustrate in the above illustration of assets correct ident cation and entry and correct figures entries above also applies to the correctness of liabilities, equities, cash flow statements, general legers, trial balance, revenue, retained earnings, expenses, percentages, interests, benefits calculations and identifications, gains, profits, debts, losses and all other areas used in accounting entries.*

# Summary

*This book contains about accounting in its pure form from the beginning to its advanced and last parts extensively. As seen in the chapters of core accounting, It entails basic and perfect accounting orientation to anyone who wants to learn about accounting in a simple and focused manner. It's about just being able to have an approach and being able to have a look into what it is with accounting. It's actually knowing about something in an introductory formant, it does not contain actual advanced details or internal advanced details of putting together accounting statements, although accounting statements are presented in advanced state for introductory discussion, as this book is a theory introduction of accounting.*

*The chapters have given a good idea of what it is about theory accounting explanation with the calculation accounts already put together in its introductory format. Accounting as it is does need very many numerous rigorous studies, mastering and practices to fully understand.*

*This book also mildly discusses accounting in finance and business. There are some accounting terms that do have meaning in accounting that are different from its other general use outside the field of accounting, some of these accounting terms are explained in accounting definitions in this book for understanding.*

*Accounting statements and reports are prepared following the generally accepted accounting principles, the current accounting standards.*

*Conceptual work in accounting follows accounting guidelines and accounting methods which are objectives of financial reports and accounting reports, qualitative method of accounting information, elements of financial statements, Measurement, and Traditional assumptions of accounting model.*

*Accountants function in very large varieties of performances in the financial accounting sector and the social sciences field. Accountants also keep the accurate records or recording of financial accounting data and reports, deals with an organisation or a firms financial operations and also individual accounting record statements where necessary. Accountants' also give financial accounting advice to the organization as financial reports for an organization management use. Often times these financial accounting advice when utilized, results in very high growth and development of the organization.*

*The term accountancy is sometimes used to refer to accounting, Accounting is the action or process of keeping financial accounts reports and accounting is the language of business. It is the system of recording and summarizing of financial transactions pertaining to a business, the process of summarizing, verifying, reporting the results and analyzing, accounting reports are used for decision making by decision makers, directors, investors, board members and governments. The financial statements that summarize the operations of an organization, the financial position of an organization and its cash flows over a particular period of time such as weekly, monthly or annually are a summary of numerous financial transactions entered into over the actual financial period being reported. Depending on an organization's management style and certain variances, a day's financial report can be created where necessary. Accounting is one of the key functions for almost any business.*

# Glossary

*Account is a type of method of recording and summarising the transactions of businesses.*

*Account in balance or Account balance is a type of account record which increases and decreases to equal the account.*

*Accounting equation is the basic equation to show the relationship in the accounts between the assets, liabilities, and owner's equity of a business.*

*Accounting period is the period that is covered in an accounts statement. Accounting period is a full year circle for an organization. Sometimes a shorter period exists. Shorter accounting periods are often a day or a week period of time, a month period and quarter periods are all shorter accounting period in comparison to the basic annual or year period of time which consists the of 12 months of the year.*

*Accounts payable account is the controlling account in the general ledger used to put together all creditors and summarise all accounts with creditors in a separate accounts payable ledger.*

*Accounts receivable account is the controlling account in the general ledger that puts together receivables and summarizes all of the accounts with customers in a separate accounts receivables ledger.*

*Accrual basis is the method of keeping accounts that shows all expenses incurred and income earned for a specified period of time, even though such expenses and income may not actually*

*have been paid or received in cash during this specified period of time. Accrual basis consists of actual income and expenses of a period of time and the anticipated income and expenses of the same period of time, all added together and subtracted together as necessary, sums the accounts of accrual basis.*

*Accrued expense is an expense incurred but has not been paid off.*

*Accrued income is income already earned but has not been collected.*

*Accrued interest is interest incurred or interest earned depending on the circumstance or type of transaction at hand and has not been paid or has not been collected depending on the type of transaction as applicable until the next period.*

*Accrued salaries are salaries that are owed to employees by employer for one period but not paid until the next.*

*Accumulated depreciation or Allowance for depreciation account is the account to which estimated depreciation accounts are added.*

*Adjusting entries are entries that are made in the general journal at the end of an accounting period to bring some accounts up to date.*

*Allowances for bad debts are the reserve for bad debts, allowance for bad debts account is the account used to show the estimated loss expected on credit granted. It can be shown as an offset against the value shown for accounts receivable.*

*Asset is whatever thing that is of value owned and used by an organization.*

*Authorised capital stock is the actual total amount of stock that a corporation is permitted to issue.*

*Bad debts are debts that are receivables in accounts receivables but are not collected or are not paid by debtors after a long period of time.*

*Bad debts collected are bad debts in accounts receivables that have been written off as not collectible but that are later paid by debtors.*

*Bad debts expense is not to be anticipated, but where it occurs, bad debts expense is the expense account to which the amount of the loss on uncollectible accounts is debited to.*

*Balance sheet is a financial report at the end of an accounting period to give a detailed actual report of the financial condition of a business as of a specific date. The balance sheet is sometimes referred to as the statement of the financial position of an organization.*

*Bank statement is a detailed record of all checks cleared and of deposits made plus the ending balance of an account with a bank.*

*Bond is a method of borrowing money through an interest bearing negotiable instrument.*

*Budget is the estimate of future income and expenditure of a specified period of time.*

*Comparative balance sheet is a balance sheet containing information for more than one accounting period, in order to use all the accounting periods' balance sheets in comparative analysis.*

*Cumulative preferred stock is a form of preferred stock that accumulates the claim for unpaid dividends from year to year.*

*Current assets or liquid assets are assets in the form of cash or are assets that can be converted to cash within a short duration of within one year.*

*Corporation business are the type of businesses that deals with Marketable securities.*

*Current liabilities refer to liabilities that are to be paid in a short period of time in a year.*

*Depreciation is the decrease in the value of fixed assets due to wear and tear, in the passage of time, and obsolescence.*

*Dividends refer to the portion of the earnings of a corporation distributed to the stockholders.*

*Equity is the value amount of a total claim against the assets of a business.*

*Expense in accounting is a decrease in ownership resulting from the operation of a business.*

*Expenses include items such as wages, rent, advertising cost, travel, delivery cost, supplies used, taxes paid, insurance purchase, repairs cost and utilities.*

*Fee is a charge that is made or paid depending on the transaction for services rendered.*

*Fixed assets are assets that are useful for more than a year period of time. Fixed assets are long term assets with a long-term durability value.*

*Fixed liabilities or long term liabilities are liabilities that are not due for payment for over a year period of time. Some long term liabilities are of Instalments payments over a long period of time, some are not to be paid by instalments payments but do have a long future due dates depending on the type of organization and depending on the item, transaction variability, and method of acquiring the account item.*

*Gain on disposal of fixed assets is the gain of income generated when a fixed asset is sold for more than its book value. The book value amount minus the actual amount which a disposal item was sold at, if there is an income generated, the income generated becomes a gain on the item in the fixed asset that is disposed.*

*Goodwill refers to intangible asset representing the difference between the book value of a business and its sale price.*

*Gross income is the total income of a business before taxes.*

*Honored is when a draft or note is paid or accepted.*

*Income is the increase in owner's equity.*

*Income statement refers to a statement that shows all the items of income, all items of expenses, and the net income or the net loss depending on the actual situation, for a specified period of time.*

*Intangible assets are assets of intangible nature such as goodwill, patents and copyrights. In the accounting structure intangible assets do appear in the assets accounts practically in instance where there are only two items of intangible assets owned by an Organization, Interest refers to the amount of money that is charged a borrower for the use of money.*

*Interest expense is the expense that is incurred for the payment of interest on any form of debt.*

*Interest income is the income realized from interest on accounts receivables and other accounts.*

*Interest rate is the percentage which shows the relationship between the interest for a specified period of time and the principal amount.*

*Investments in assets accounts are investments in securities, land held for future site and other form of investments that are purchased for future appreciation.*

*Liability refers to an amount that is owed such as debts, accounts payables, and long term debts or long term liabilities.*

*Liquid assets or current assets are assets in the form of cash or are assets that can be converted to cash within a short duration of within one year.*

*Liquidation is the process of selling all assets of a business to pay liabilities, with any remaining funds distributed within the owners of the business.*

*Long term liabilities or fixed liabilities are liabilities that are not due for payment for over a year period of time.*

*Market value refers to the actual value amount at which a share of stock can be sold at a specific time.*

*Maturity value is the amount that is to be paid when a note becomes due with interest or without interest.*

*Miscellaneous entries are entries that are not to be recorded in a special journal and are recorded in the general journal.*

*Net income is the difference derived when income is larger than expense.*

*Net loss is the difference in decrease when expenses are larger than income.*

*Operating expenses refers to the costs that are incurred by a business that shows a decrease in the ownership with exception of expenses incurred represented by the cost of goods sold.*

*Operating income refers to the increase in owner's equity of a business from its principal operations.*

*Owner's' equity accounts is the capital equity summary comprising of retained earnings, net income and drawings or withdrawer by the owner. Sometimes depending on the organization the equity includes stock dividends and dividends, various stocks such as preferred stocks, common stocks and their percentages and price per value.*

*Partnership business is a type of business organization in which two or more persons come together to form a business and share in operating the business together in agreement and share profits or losses of the business.*

*Payee is a person or a business that a payment is paid.*

*Payroll refers to a list of employees that are entitled to payments of salaries or wages for a particular period with the amounts of each employee of all employees on the list.*

*Payroll taxes or employment taxes are taxes collected on salaries and wages of employees.*

*Petty cash fund is an amount of money that is kept on hand for making payments of small amounts of cash to operate a business or for use.*

*Reconciliation statement is the actual balanced reconciliation statement after the process of bringing into agreement the balance of a bank statement and the balance on check stubs.*

*Retained earnings are the amount of money that is earned by a business and is in hold in the business and not given out as earnings but kept as surplus earnings or accumulated earnings.*

*Revenue refers to the inflow of assets which result from conducting the activities of a business.*

*Revenue expenditure refers to a certain expense or expenditure that do not increase the value of a fixed asset but which is useful in maintaining the asset in good operating condition.*

*Sales budget refers to the estimate of the income anticipated from sales for some future period of time.*

*Sales tax is the tax a seller of commodity must collect on sales to customers and in turn remit the sales tax to the government as applicable.*

*Salvage value is the amount for which a fixed asset is sold at the end of its approximated useful period.*

*Solvency is a company's ability to pay up debts as at when due.*

*Stakeholders are those who own part of a business capital or part of a working capital of a film.*

*Statement of account refers to a form which is sent to a customer that shows charges to the customer account with amounts credited to the account and showing the balance of the account.*

*Stock certificate is a document evidence of a stockholder's ownership in a corporation.*

*Stockholders refer to the individuals who own one or more shares of stock in an organization often time a corporation type of organization.*

*Stockholders equity is the capital stocks account summary comprising of retained earnings, stock dividends and dividends, various stocks such as preferred stocks, common stocks and their percentages and price per value.*

*Subsidiary ledger refers to a separate ledger summarized in a single controlling account in the general ledger.*

*Terms of sale refers to the agreement made between the buyer and the seller as to what manner of payment to be used in the transaction and the delivery of commodities.*

*Trade discount is the deduction in price from the list of price.*

*Trial balance is the proof of the equality of debits and credits in the ledger.*

*Unit record is a card that contains one complete record.*

*Voucher system refers to a method of controlling disbursements of cash providing that a form be prepared and approved before cash payment is made.*

*Withdrawals are assets taken from the business by the owner of a business for personal use.*

*Worksheet refers to an analysis paper that shows provision for sorting and interpreting the trial balance on a single sheet of paper from which the income statement and balance sheet are prepared.*